EXTREME PLACES

The
Longest
River

Other books in the Extreme Places series include:

The Deepest Lake
The Highest Mountain
The Longest Bridge

EXTREME PLACES

The Longest River

Darv Johnson

KIDHAVEN PRESS™

THOMSON

GALE

San Diego • Detroit • New York • San Francisco • Cleveland
New Haven, Conn. • Waterville, Maine • London • Munich

For more information, contact
KidHaven Press
27500 Drake Rd.
Farmington Hills, MI 48331-3535
Or you can visit our Internet site at http://www.gale.com

LIBRARY OF CONGRESS CATALOGING-IN-PUBLICATION DATA

Johnson, Darv, 1971–
    The longest river / by Darv Johnson.
        v. cm. — (Extreme places)
Includes bibliographical references and index.
Summary: Discusses the path of the Nile River, the plants and animals found
around it, historical expeditions, and the future of the river.
Contents: Following the river Nile—Plants and animals of the Nile—The search
for the source—A river under pressure.
    ISBN 0-7377-1417-4
    1. Nile River Valley—Juvenile literature. [1. Nile River. 2. Nile River Valley.]
I. Title. II. Series.
    DT115 .J64 2003
    962—dc21

                                                                2002007595

Contents

Following the Nile River

The world's longest river plunges down waterfalls, plods through swamps, crosses a desert, and hurdles a giant dam on its journey to the sea. It provides water for crops, turns turbines to make electricity, and makes a watery home for hippos and crocodiles. The world's longest river is called the Nile, and it begins as a trickling stream high in the mountains of central Africa.

Other rivers are bigger or more powerful than the Nile. The Amazon River in South America, for example, is two hundred miles wide where it meets the ocean. But the Nile River's path from central Africa to the Mediterranean Sea is 4,150 miles long—longer than the

A felucca, a traditional Egyptian boat, sails on the Nile, the world's longest river.

distance from New York to California, and longer than any other river in the world.

The Journey North

The Nile travels in a different style from the other great rivers of the world. Instead of moving from north to south, the slope of the land takes it in the opposite direction. This backward trip begins at the most distant source of Nile water, a small spring that bubbles out of the ground in the tiny nation of Burundi. From here the waters rush through Tanzania and Rwanda before feeding into a giant lake called Lake Victoria.

By the time the river spills out the north shore of the lake, it has passed over the **equator**, the imaginary line that divides Earth's Northern and Southern Hemispheres. This section of the river, which crosses the nation of Uganda, is known as the Victoria Nile. The Victoria Nile tumbles down out of the mountains into another large lake, called Lake Albert, and then empties out the other side.

The Swampy Sudd

The river widens and slows as it crosses over the Ugandan border into the Sudan. After the city of Juba, it passes into a broad plain lined by rolling hills. The entire plain floods in the rainy season, creating a swamp the size of England.

This swampy stretch of the Nile is called the Sudd, or "the barrier." The sluggish river splits into many branches and channels. Tall grasses and water hyacinth, a purple-flowered plant, choke it at every turn. Giant islands of vegetation break off and float downstream.

The weeds clog the river and make it difficult for boats to pass. In 1880 Italian explorer Romolo Gessi tried to travel north through the Sudd with six hundred men. He found his ship's path blocked at every turn by thick grasses and weeds. Trapped for months, the men began to starve. Gessi was one of the few to survive.

Just Add Water

Without the help of **tributaries**—smaller streams and rivers that supply larger ones with water—the Nile would dry up long before it reached the Mediterranean. More than three-quarters of its water comes from smaller rivers in the Ethiopian highlands. These rivers swell with heavy rains and melting snow every summer, and then add that bounty of water to the Nile.

The Nile's first major tributary is called the Sobat River. It flows into the Nile just above the city of Malakal. For the next five hundred miles, the river is known as the White Nile—a wide, calm river lined with swamps.

The second major source of the Nile is anything but calm. The Blue Nile starts in the mountains of Ethiopia, a mile above sea level. The Blue Nile plunges through a mile-deep canyon in its rush to meet the White Nile. The cliff walls above the canyon close together to block out the sun. The river hauls a heavy load of **sediment**, suspended particles of soil and sand that color the water.

The Blue and White Niles meet in the Sudanese city of Khartoum—a word that means "elephant's trunk." The place where the two rivers meet resembles the outline of the animal's head, with the Blue Nile forming the trunk.

Pouring from the mountains of Ethiopia, the Blue Nile rushes over a waterfall on its way to meet the White Nile.

The two rivers do not mix right away. They flow side by side down the same riverbed, kept apart by the different sediment loads they carry. They finally meld into one waterway after several miles. The journey to the sea is halfway done.

Rough River Riding

Fifty miles north of Khartoum, the river boils over the Sixth **Cataract**, a long series of rapids caused by rocks that have pushed their way to the surface of the river. The Nile passes over five more cataracts before it reaches the Mediterranean Sea. The rocky, rough waters make it difficult for boats to travel up or down the river.

The Making of the Nile

The Atbara River meets the Nile 150 miles after the Sixth Cataract. Like the Blue Nile, the Atbara begins in the Ethiopian mountains. It is here, scientists believe, that the Nile started about 30 million years ago. The Sudd was then a self-contained lake to the South. According to one theory, sediments built up in Lake Sudd, shrinking the lake and spilling water over its edge to the north. That water created a riverbed that joined the two separate river systems into the single, long Nile River.

Across the Desert

Today, the waters of the Atbara River are the boost the Nile needs to make it across eight hundred miles of desert. On the hot sands, the temperature often soars above one hundred degrees, and it rains less than an inch a year. The only glimpses of green in this vast desert are the crops growing in thin strips along the river.

The dry stretch ends with a splash at Lake Nasser, which straddles the border of the Sudan and Egypt. Nasser, the world's second-largest man-made lake, was formed by the construction of the Aswan Dam in the 1960s. It buries the Nile for three hundred miles until the river tumbles over the dam, free again.

To the Sea

The river must travel five hundred more miles from the dam to the Egyptian capital of Cairo, the largest city in Africa. Along the way, it passes by the great pyramids, giant

A painting depicts a woman gathering plants along the Nile River with the great pyramids in the background.

The Nile River flows through Cairo, the largest city in Africa and the capital of Egypt.

tombs built thousands of years ago to house the mummies, or preserved remains, of great kings.

The river winds through bustling Cairo, crowded with diesel engine barges and ferries, and graceful flat-bottomed sailing ships called feluccas. Next, it splits into two smaller rivers called the Rosetta and the Damietta. They, in turn, fan out into the wedge-shaped Nile **Delta**. Built from rich soil washed out of the Ethiopian mountains, the delta is some of the best farmland in all of Africa. One hundred miles later, the Nile washes gently into the Mediterranean Sea. The river's long journey is complete.

Plants and Animals of the Nile River

In the mountains where the Nile begins, the weather is mild and the rain is plentiful. Jungles grow along the river banks. The forests are thick with banana and rubber trees, coffee plants, and bamboo.

As the river drops out of the mountains, the rainfall and vegetation are less common. The forests become thinner. Soon the Nile is passing through **savannas**, fields

The Nile River rushes over steep cliffs and through deep canyons toward the desert.

of tall grass and a few hardy trees such as the baobab. The baobab has few branches on top and spreads out as it reaches the ground. It looks as if it has been planted up-side down. Its trunk can reach thirty feet around. Native people hollow out the trunk and use it for water storage or temporary shelter.

Even the trees disappear as the climate becomes drier. Small, hardy shrubs take their place. When the Nile enters the desert, where years may pass without rain, there is no permanent vegetation at all.

Because the Nile flows through a wide range of climates and **ecosystems**, the river and its banks are home to a wide variety of animals. Some of the creatures live under the water and are difficult to spot. Others are so big that they are difficult to miss.

The Enormous, Endangered Rhino

Only elephants are bigger than the white rhino, one of two kinds of rhino that drink, splash, and cool themselves in the Nile. The creatures weigh about twice as much as the average car, and they're almost as fast. The African black rhino, which also lives on the Nile, can reach speeds of thirty miles per hour.

Rhinos usually leave humans alone, but they are known to have bad tempers in breeding season. Fortunately, the creatures are **herbivores** that survive on a steady diet of plants. The white rhino's massive square lips are perfect for mowing huge amounts of grass growing along the Nile.

Both types of rhino are distinguished by the large horns on their snout. The horn is made of a hardened

A rhino, distinguished by a large horn made of hardened hairlike material, grazes on dried grass.

hairlike material and can weigh up to ten pounds. Some cultures believe the horn has medicinal value. In pursuit of this prize, hunters have made rhinos one of the most endangered species.

Hungry Hippos

A hippopotamus is almost as big as a rhino. Hippos are barrel-shaped animals that can be fifteen feet long and weigh up to three tons.

Hippos are excellent swimmers despite their size. They can stay underwater for as long as ten minutes. They spend the day splashing in the Nile to stay cool, gathering in groups of up to fifteen animals. A baby

Two large hippos spar in the cool Nile waters.

hippo, which can weigh more than a hundred pounds at birth, hitches a ride on its mother's back.

At night, hippos, with their stubby legs, climb out of the river to forage for grass. They do not wander far, however. It is rare to find a hippo more than a mile or two from the Nile.

The Nile Crocodile

Nile crocodiles stay close to the river, too. Baby crocodiles hatch from their eggs at the river's edge, and they stay hidden there until they are large enough to be safe from hungry birds, fish, and bigger crocodiles. The world's largest **reptile**, a crocodile may grow up to twenty feet long. Scientists believe that crocodiles of that size may be more than a hundred years old.

In the daytime, Nile crocodiles are easy to spot. They sun themselves on sandbars in the river, opening and closing their jaws to stay cool. But at night, when crocodiles are most active, they are almost invisible.

Hungry crocodiles wait motionless on the shore for birds or small mammals to pass. Crocodiles might look slow and clumsy on land, but they have been known to reach speeds of up to thirty miles per hour.

Sometimes they slide into the river on their bellies and drift like logs. Because their nostrils, eyes, and ear openings are high on their heads, crocodiles keep most of their bodies hidden underwater. They strike first with their long, heavy tails, knocking their prey into the water. Powerful jaws and cone-shaped teeth finish the job. If the meal is too big to devour at one sitting, crocs store the remains

Lunging above the water, a Nile crocodile chomps a large mullet in its powerful jaws.

in their burrows, small cavelike nests tunneled into the mud at the edge of the river.

Birds of the Nile

Crocodiles mark their territory with roars so fierce that their heads and tails whip out of the water with the strain. But the fearsome noise does not scare off the crocodile bird. It stays close to the crocodile, picking over the creature's tough hide, or skin, for parasites to eat. When trouble approaches, the bird warns the crocodile with its cries.

Several other birds make their home on the Nile. One is the whale-headed stork. As tall as a child and resembling a pelican, the bird has a thick bill perfect for cracking open turtle shells, one of the stork's favorite meals.

Two other Nile birds are the red-billed ibis and the crowned crane. With a long bill and great balance, the red-billed ibis perches on branches at the river's edge, waiting for fish to dart past. The crowned crane, meanwhile, fishes in the shallow water. The bird gets its name because of the "crown" on its head made of spiky golden feathers.

The masked weaver also lives up to its name. The small bird gathers hundreds of blades of grass to make its sock-shaped nest. It then weaves the grass together with its beak and feet.

Under the Surface

Another world of life exists under the Nile's surface. The red-tailed Nile catfish lives in the mud on the river bottom, using its long whiskers to feel its way through the darkness. It feeds on whatever food filters down through the water—but humans do not feed on it. Unlike people in other parts of the world, few Nile residents believe the catfish is suitable for eating.

Also found in the Nile is the tilapia, which has a curious approach to raising its offspring. The parents hold

Known for the spiky golden feathers on top of its head, a crowned crane wades off the bank of the Nile looking for food.

the newborn fish in their mouths to **incubate** them, or keep them safe until they are larger. When the young fish are old enough, the parents release them into the river. Because of this odd behavior, the tilapia also goes by the name of the Egyptian mouth-breeder.

The biggest fish in the river, and one of the biggest in the world, is the Nile perch. It can tip the scales at three hundred pounds and reach six feet in length. The fast-growing fish has been a source of food for river people for centuries.

Arid desert and plants line large stretches of the Nile River.

In Hostile Terrain

When the Nile reaches the desert, what life there is to be found is largely underwater. That's because the plants, shrubs, and grasses that lined the Nile for so many miles have been replaced by sand. In this forbidding environment, where food and water are scarce and rain never comes, only a handful of hardy creatures can survive. Often, Arabian camels are the only creatures visible from the river on the miles of shifting sands.

The Search for the Source

Before the Nile earned the title of the world's longest river, explorers first had to find its source. But exactly where the Nile began remained shrouded in myth and mystery for thousands of years.

The earliest quests took place more than two thousand years ago, when Egypt was absorbed into the Roman Empire. The Roman emperor Nero sent a group of his soldiers to find the source of the river that watered Egypt, but they abandoned the journey after encountering the confusing swamps of the Sudd.

One after another as the centuries passed, explorers set out into the uncharted wilds of Africa, seeking the glory that would belong to the discoverer of the source. Some of them simply got lost. Others were turned back by exhaustion, disease, hostile tribes, and impassable swamps and rapids. "Of the source of the Nile no one

Nero, emperor of Rome, sent soldiers to look for the source of the Nile more than two thousand years ago.

can give any account,"[1] wrote the Greek scholar Herodotus in 460 B.C. after the cataracts at Aswan forced him to abandon his own exploration.

It was not until the nineteenth century, after the quest for the source had become an obsession of European empires, that explorers stumbled close to the truth.

Burton and Speke

Irishman Sir Richard Burton and John Hanning Speke, a British army officer, were no strangers to the perils of African exploration. On their 1854 expedition to the continent's northeast coast, the two men were attacked by Somali warriors. A javelin wounded Burton in the cheek. Speke was captured, tied to the ground, and beaten with clubs before managing to escape.

This brush with death did not put a stop to the two men's African journeys. In 1857 they set out in search of the source of the Nile.

After assembling a large **caravan** of guides and supplies, Burton and Speke traveled west from the island of Zanzibar across Tanzania on a route used by Arab slave traders. Tales of a giant interior lake, rumored to be the source, drew them onward. They traveled through land that few Europeans had ever seen, encountering caravans of ivory and livestock headed for coastal trading posts. They scared up herds of zebras and bounding antelopes, and they met with African kings and queens who had never seen Europeans before.

The fierce environment held many hazards for the expedition. Burton and Speke had to face down tribes that demanded *hongo*, a toll paid by travelers for the right to pass through their lands. Tropical diseases took their toll as well. Burton became so sick that he had to be carried, and Speke was temporarily blinded.

When Burton became too ill to lead the expedition, he handed command over to Speke, who pushed on toward what he hoped was the source. Finally, in 1858,

Speke reached the southern shore of a giant, shallow lake he named Victoria. Based on the lake's size and location, he guessed that this must be the source of the Nile. But he ran out of supplies and was forced to return to England before he could find proof.

Sir Richard Burton (left) and John Hanning Speke (right) endured hardships at the hands of natives and tropical diseases in their quest for the source of the Nile.

Looking for Proof

Speke vowed to return and in 1860, he did. This time he was in command of his own expedition, funded by England's Royal Geographical Society. He reached the northern shore of Lake Victoria in 1862. There he found Ripon Falls, the outlet through which the Nile cascaded from the lake toward the Mediterranean Sea. Though tribal war prevented him from following the river north, he believed he had found proof of the source.

"I saw that old father Nile without any doubt rises in the Victoria,"[2] Speke wrote from the lake's shores.

While Speke had no doubts, others did. One of the doubters was his fellow explorer Richard Burton, who believed that the Nile arose in many lakes, rather than only one. Once friends, the two men waged a bitter public dispute over the source of the Nile. In 1864, the British Association for the Advancement of Science arranged for the two men to argue their sides in a public debate. Before the debate could take place, however, Speke was killed in a hunting accident. It fell to other explorers to find proof.

"Dr. Livingstone, I Presume?"

One of the explorers was David Livingstone, a Scottish doctor and missionary turned explorer with ideas of his own about the source of the Nile. In 1866 he set out into the heart of Africa with a party of sixty to look for the source. He promptly disappeared.

All trace of Livingstone was lost for years. Men who had deserted him early in his expedition claimed that he was dead. Search parties sent out by the Royal Geographical Society, which had sponsored his travels, returned empty-handed.

In the end it was Henry Stanley, a reporter sent by an American newspaper, who found Livingstone. After a brutal eight-month march in 1871, Stanley found the lost explorer alive at Lake Tanganyika, deep in the African wilderness. Livingstone had wandered too far south in his search for the source and fallen ill with fever. Stanley greeted him with the famous words, "Dr. Livingstone, I presume?"[3]

Stanley returned from the rescue mission a hero; and he had a huge story for his newspaper. But although he was battered by disease, Livingstone refused to leave Africa. He died there in 1873, still trying to prove his own theory of the source.

The Final Link

A mapping expedition launched by British general Charles George Gordon in 1874 finally confirmed Speke's belief that Lake Victoria was the main source of the Nile. For a time, it was assumed that the source was no farther south.

But the search was not quite finished. Later adventurers traced the source of the Nile back even farther, to small tributaries in the countries of Burundi and Rwanda that feed Lake Victoria.

In 1937 German explorer Burkhart Waldecker found the main tributary of Victoria. He followed its path upstream to a small spring in Burundi, one of the smallest

A painting depicts the famous meeting between Henry Stanley (right) and Dr. David Livingstone.

countries in the world. Today, the spot is marked by a small pyramid with a bronze plaque bearing the Latin inscription CAPUT NILI—THE SOURCE OF THE NILE.

A River Under Pressure

For millions of years, the Nile has flowed without ceasing from mountains to sea. And for thousands of years, the people who have lived along it have used its waters to quench their thirst and bring their crops to life.

Today, the changes caused by that long connection between humans and river are visible everywhere along its length. Upstream, weeds have invaded, choking the waterway. There are also invisible invaders in the water: mercury, lead, and other types of pollution from pesticides and fertilizers. The conditions are difficult for many types of fish, and fewer species than ever swim the waters of the Nile.

Downstream, too, the river has changed. The water that delivered nutrient-rich mud to the Nile Delta is now silt free, and the delta is shrinking as a result. Borg-el-Borellos, once a village on the Mediterranean coast of

Egypt, is now underwater and abandoned. Long years of hard use have affected the health of the river.

Water Withdrawals

At first, human use of the Nile was gentle. It began more than five thousand years ago, as residents of the Nile basin waited for the river's annual flood. Year after year, farmers planted seeds in the rich layers of mud the floodwaters left behind. They counted on the high water

Farmers living on the banks of the Nile find their way of life threatened by the receding water levels of the river.

Ancient Egyptians monitor the levels of the Nile after a flood on a nilometer, a scale carved on a tall column.

to **irrigate** their crops and allow them to grow in the dry climate. So important was the flood that ancient Egyptians recorded the river level with nilometers—scales cut into rocks or stone walls.

Depending on the flood was risky, however. If the river was too high, the fields got too much water and crops suffered. If the river was too low, crops could not grow at all, and the people suffered as **famine** gripped the land. At the same time, the annual flood limited the growing season to only a third of the year. The people of the Nile realized that to control their own destinies, they would have to learn to control the river.

Harnessing the Nile

Early attempts to harness the river produced crude machines for drawing out small amounts of water. The triple shadoof, for example, dips buckets into the river like a bird dipping its beak. Another machine, the Archimedes screw, is a hand-driven machine for raising water up. Although their designs are centuries old, both of these devices are still used along the Nile today.

Egyptian farmers use an Archimedes screw to irrigate their crops along the Nile Delta.

Egyptians also developed the technique of basin irrigation. They learned how to divert river water into a large basin, where it deposited a load of silt for crops. The water then drained into a series of lower basins, slightly downstream, until finally it was allowed back into the Nile.

As technology improved, so, too, did the water-control projects. In the 1920s a maze of canals and dams called the Gezira Scheme turned a large swath of the Sudan into farmable land. And in the 1960s Egypt broke ground on a construction project that dwarfed anything else on the Nile.

The Aswan Dam

The Aswan Dam took more than a decade to build. Two miles long and a half mile wide at its base, the Aswan blocked the Nile's journey to the sea. The river backed up behind the dam, forming a three-hundred-mile-long **reservoir** called Lake Nasser—one of the largest artificial lakes in the world. Humans can control how much of that water flows past the dam by flipping switches and pressing buttons.

In many ways, the Aswan project is a success. Spun by the force of the Nile, whirling turbines within the dam's walls now generate about a quarter of Egypt's electricity. The giant Lake Nasser stores several years' worth of water, meaning Egypt has less to fear from drought than its neighbors.

The pumps and canals fed by the reservoir have allowed Egypt to turn millions of acres that were once

Hundreds of generators line the top of the Aswan Dam, which produces one-quarter of Egypt's electricity.

desert into farmland. At the same time, farmers can water their fields year-round, which means that two or three crops can be grown every year instead of only one. The nation is no longer at the mercy of the flood.

The Cost of Control

Control of the Nile has come at a cost, however. It can be measured in pollution and weeds, a shrinking delta, and fewer kinds of fish.

Every project built to harness the Nile alters the river's natural state. Giant dams, for example, block the free passage of fish species that used to migrate up and down the river. Before the Aswan was built, forty-seven fish species lived in the river. Ten years after the dam was finished, only seventeen species remained.

Dams also slow the river down. The silt the river carries—the silt that once created the rich farmland of the Nile Delta—now falls to the bottom of canals and reservoirs. Without it, the delta is wasting away, shrinking by several hundred feet a year in places.

Meanwhile, lack of silt lets more sunlight into the river. The added sunlight allows weeds to grow faster, clogging the Nile. The situation is made worse by the loss of the annual flood that once flushed weeds out into the Mediterranean Sea.

Workers harvest sugarcane where nutrient-rich silt once flooded the Nile Delta.

A plant in Egypt produces chemical fertilizers to aid in desert farming.

The loss of the flood has also changed farming along the Nile. Farmers can no longer depend on an annual deposit of mud from the river to fertilize their crops. Instead, they have to rely on artificial fertilizers, many of which contain harmful chemicals.

Even the longer growing season has a downside. Because farmers are growing more, they use more fertilizers and pesticides. These substances find their way back into the river and pose threats to animals and humans alike.

Looking Forward

Demand for the Nile's precious water is certain to grow in the years ahead. Egypt already uses about 98 percent of the Nile water that reaches the country's southern border, and its population is growing by about a million people every nine months.

At the same time, upstream nations such as the Sudan and Uganda are making plans to increase their own withdrawals from the Nile. A total of 160 million people from ten African nations live in the river basin. That number will double by 2025, according to experts.

The bigger population will need more drinking water, more food, and more electricity—and it will turn to the Nile to supply these needs. New projects that will use more river water are already being developed. In 1997, for example, Egypt began construction of the world's most powerful pumping station. The pump will be able to suck sixty-six thousand gallons of water per second out of Lake Nasser and deliver it to farmers.

The challenge ahead for Egypt and the other nations of the Nile is to use the river's resources wisely. The health of the world's longest river depends, in large part, on the ability of humans to control their thirst for its water.

Notes

1. Quoted in Robert Caputo, "Journey Up the Nile," *National Geographic,* May 1985, p. 629.

2. Quoted in Giovanni Guadalupi, *The Discovery of the Nile.* New York: Stewart, Tabori and Chang, 1997, p. 160.

3. Quoted in Guadalupi, *The Discovery of the Nile,* p. 197.

Glossary

caravan: A company of travelers, animals, and supplies, moving together for safety.

cataract: A large waterfall.

delta: Flat land, usually triangular, formed by deposits of soil and sand at the mouth of a large river.

ecosystems: Communities of plants, animals, and bacteria, and their physical environment.

equator: The imaginary line that divides Earth's Northern and Southern Hemispheres.

famine: A shortage of food.

herbivore: An animal that eats only plants.

incubate: To keep offspring in a safe environment for development.

irrigate: To provide an artificial supply of water to farmland.

reptile: A class of cold-blooded animals including snakes, lizards, turtles, and crocodiles.

reservoir: A lake or pond where water is collected and stored for use.

savannas: Grassy plains with scattered trees.

sediment: Soil or sand that settles to the bottom of a river.

tributaries: Streams or rivers that add their waters to a larger one.

For Further Exploration

Books

Giovanni Guadalupi, *The Discovery of the Nile.* New York: Stewart, Tabori and Chang, 1997. This book offers an illustrated history of the explorers who searched for the source of the Nile.

Geoffrey Moorhouse, *The Nile.* London: Barrie & Jenkins Limited, 1989. In a series of stunning photographs, this book captures the Nile and the people and animals that live along it.

Virginia Morrell, *Blue Nile: Ethiopia's River of Magic and Mystery.* Washington: National Geographic Society, 2001. The author journeys by raft down the Blue Nile, from Ethiopia to the Sudanese border.

Michael Pollard, *The Nile.* Tarrytown, NY: Benchmark, 2000. In words, photos, and illustrations, this book depicts the river's history, culture, and wildlife.

John Hanning Speke, *The Journal of the Discovery of the Source of the Nile*, Meneola, NY: Dover, 1996. British explorer Speke's 1863 account of his journey to the shores of Lake Victoria in 1858.

Periodicals

Robert Caputo, "Journey Up the Nile," *National Geographic,*

May 1985. The author travels by land and river to the source of the Nile. Contains excellent maps and photographs.

Websites

Crocodiles! (www.pbs.org). This site offers a page on the crocodile, a species that has survived almost unchanged since the time of the dinosaurs.

The Nile (www.school.discovery.com). This site provides lesson plans for sixth- to eighth-grade teachers, along with photographic guides to the plants and animals of the Nile.

Wild Egypt—The Nile Adventure (www.touregypt.net). This website takes viewers on a virtual safari down the Nile River.

Index

Picture Credits

About the Author

Darv Johnson is a writer who lives and works in New Orleans. He has previously written about the Amazon rain forest and Ronald Reagan for Lucent Books.